RACIAL JUSTICE in AMERICA
EXCELLENCE AND ACHIEVEMENT

EXCELLENCE in STEM

HEDREICH NICHOLS with KELISA WING

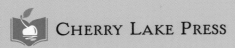
CHERRY LAKE PRESS

Published in the United States of America by Cherry Lake Publishing Group
Ann Arbor, Michigan
www.cherrylakepublishing.com

Reading Adviser: Beth Walker Gambro, MS, Ed., Reading Consultant, Yorkville, IL
Content Adviser: Kelisa Wing
Book Design and Cover Art: Felicia Macheske

Photo Credits: © Daisy Daisy/Shutterstock.com, 5; Library of Congress, Reproduction of page from notebook of Leonardo da Vinci, LOC Control No: 2006681086, 7; © Archive PL/Alamy Stock Photo, 9; © adike/Shutterstock.com, 10; NASA, Glenn Research Center, 13; United States Air Force, 15; © Kajohnwit Boonsom/Shutterstock.com, 19; Library of Congress Gift; Col. Godwin Ordway; 1948. LOC Control No: 2014645761, 21; Library of Congress, Stereograph, G. Eric and Edith Matson Photograph Collection LOC Control No: 2019699853, 22; Engraving by William J. Simmons, New York Public Library: *digitalcollections.nypl.org/items/510d47da-735d-a3d9-e040-e00a18064a99*, 22; Kano Computing, flickr.com/photos/118284351@N02/12678894163/in/photostream/CC BY-SA 2.0, 25; © Dr. Tai-Danae Bradley, notes by used with permission, 27; © Suwatchai Pluemruetai/Shutterstock.com, 30; © Natykach Nataliia/Shutterstock.com, 30

Graphics Throughout: © debra hughes/Shutterstock.com; © Galyna_P/Shutterstock.com; © olllikeballoon/Shutterstock.com

Cherry Lake Press is an imprint of Cherry Lake Publishing Group.

Library of Congress Cataloging-in-Publication Data

Names: Nichols, Hedreich, author. | Wing, Kelisa, author.
Title: Excellence in STEM / by Hedreich Nichols, Kelisa Wing.
Description: Ann Arbor, Michigan : Cherry Lake Publishing, [2022] | Series: Racial justice in America: excellence and achievement | Audience: Grades 7-9 | Summary: "Students will learn about some of the inventions and discoveries Black men and women have made in the world of STEM. From Dr. Marie Maynard Daly to Dr. Tai-Danae Bradley, some of the many ways Black people have contributed to our country's science and technology are explored. The Racial Justice in America: Excellence and Achievement series celebrates Black achievement and culture, while exploring racism in a comprehensive, honest, and age-appropriate way. Developed in conjunction with educator, advocate, and author Kelisa Wing to reach children of all races and encourage them to approach our history with open eyes and minds. Books include 21st Century Skills and content, activities created by Wing, table of contents, glossary, index, author biography, sidebars, and educational matter"—Provided by publisher.
Identifiers: LCCN 2021047060 | ISBN 9781534199323 (hardcover) | ISBN 9781668900468 (paperback) | ISBN 9781668906224 (ebook) | ISBN 9781668901908 (pdf)
Subjects: LCSH: Discoveries in science—Juvenile literature. | African Americans—Juvenile literature. | Race discrimination—Juvenile literature.
Classification: LCC Q180.55.D57 N53 2022 | DDC 507.1/2—dc23/eng/20211108
LC record available at https://lccn.loc.gov/2021047060

Cherry Lake Publishing Group would like to acknowledge the work of the Partnership for 21st Century Learning, a Network of Battelle for Kids. Please visit *http://www.battelleforkids.org/networks/p21* for more information.

Printed in the United States of America
Corporate Graphics

Hedreich Nichols, author, educator, and host of the YouTube series on equity #SmallBites, is a retired Grammy-nominated singer-songwriter turned EdTech teacher who uses her experience as a "one Black friend" to help others understand race, equity, and how to celebrate diversity. When not educating and advocating, she enjoys making music with her son, multi-instrumentalist @SwissChrisOnBass.

Kelisa Wing honorably served in the U.S. Army and has been an educator for 14 years. She is the author of *Promises and Possibilities: Dismantling the School to Prison Pipeline*, *If I Could: Lessons for Navigating an Unjust World*, and *Weeds & Seeds: How to Stay Positive in the Midst of Life's Storms*. She speaks both nationally and internationally about discipline reform, equity, and student engagement. Kelisa lives in Northern Virginia with her husband and two children.

Introduction
What Is STEM? | Page 4

Chapter 1
S Is for Science | Page 6

Chapter 2
T Is for Technology | Page 14

Chapter 3
E Is for Engineering | Page 18

Chapter 4
M Is for Math | Page 26

Making a Way Out of NO WAY!!! | Page 31

Extend Your Learning | Page 32

Glossary | Page 32

Index | Page 32

What Is STEM?

STEM is an acronym for **S**cience, **T**echnology, **E**ngineering, and **M**ath. These are all important fields that impact our lives every day. People who work in STEM fields keep us healthy, allow us to communicate, help us to get from one place to another, measure things, count money—and solve all kinds of problems. Even before we called these fields STEM, important people in science, technology, engineering, and math made many advancements that have helped to shape our world today. While you may not have learned about the Black men and women who have excelled in STEM fields, it certainly doesn't mean there haven't been any. In this book, you will learn about some of those people.

Inventors often get their start exploring STEM fields.

CHAPTER 1

S Is for Science

What's the difference between a wolf and a dog? Why is soda fizzy? Why do I have to eat vegetables? What is the Sun made of? Where do rainbows come from and where do they end?

If you have ever asked any questions about the world around you, you owe the answers to science. Science gives us answers to questions about ourselves and the world around us. Scientists are the people who do the research to give us the answers to our questions.

There are all types of scientists. Hundreds and hundreds of years ago, there were no schools and universities for science. Scientists were just curious people who liked to find out how things worked or find answers to unanswered questions. Many were great observers who took notes that led to more questions than answers.

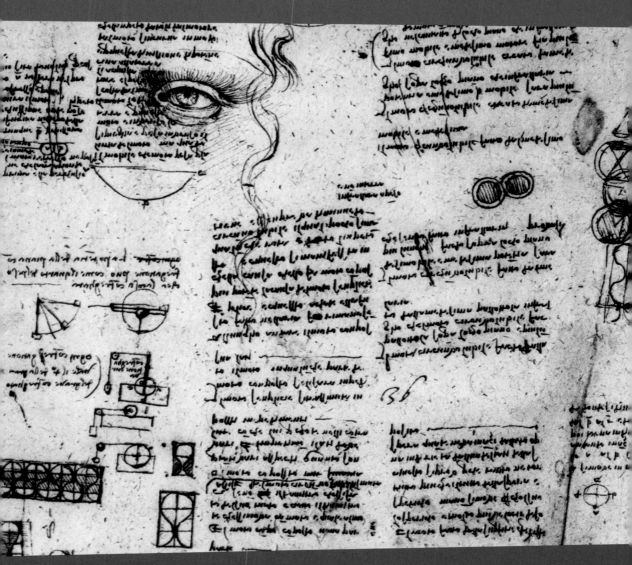

Leonardo da Vinci was an artist and a scientist ahead of his time.

Now, people go to school to become scientists. Some go to specialized schools for many years to learn methods to ask questions and test their answers. They write papers and books so that other people can read about the answers they find.

One person who liked to find answers to questions was Marie Maynard Daly. Daly was born in 1921. In her time, not a lot of women went to college, especially Black women. Her father, who loved chemistry and didn't get the chance to complete his own studies, encouraged her to go to college. Daly graduated top of her class at Queen's College. She went on to get her doctorate from Columbia University in New York. A doctorate is a degree that you can earn in about 3 years after a bachelor's and master's degree. People who earn this degree earn a PhD and are called doctors of their field. A person with this degree is different than a medical doctor. Many scientists have a PhD in their field.

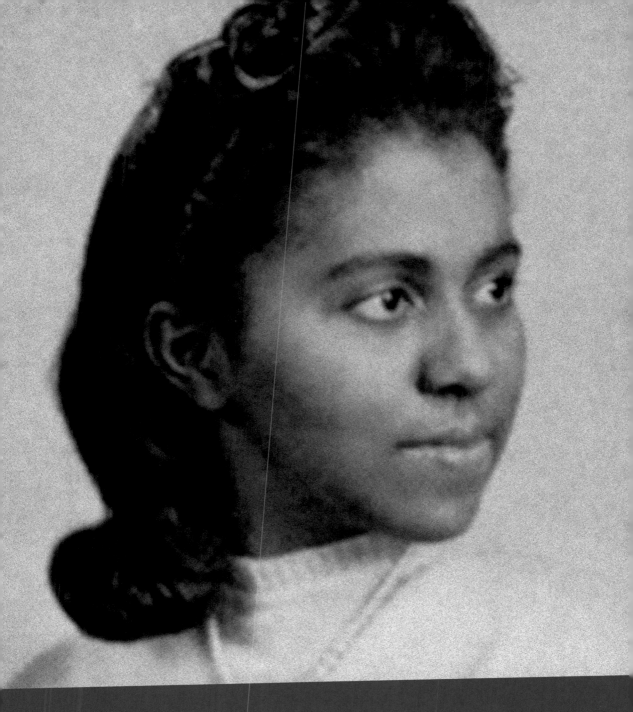

Dr. Daly was the first Black woman in the United States to earn a PhD in chemistry.

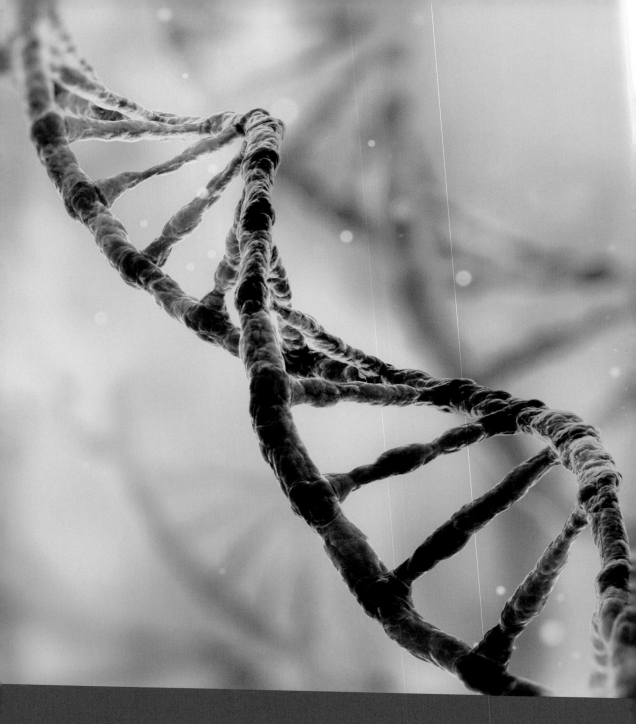

Deoxyribonucleic acid or DNA carries instructions for all life. Every living organism has DNA.

Dr. Daly was important to science because, even though she wasn't a medical doctor, she studied many things about how our bodies work. She studied the effects of smoking on the heart and lungs. She studied how cholesterol causes arteries to get clogged. Maybe most importantly, she helped us understand how DNA is organized in cells.

Dr. Daly was a groundbreaking scientist and an activist. She saw how few Black women were in science careers. She worked to create opportunities for other Black women who wanted to study science.

Another important Black scientist is Julian Manly Earls. Besides earning 10 university degrees, Dr. Earls was known for several firsts at NASA. During 40 years of working there, he became the first Black office chief, division chief, and deputy director. As a health physics expert, he also wrote NASA's first health physics guide, which helps keep people safe when working around **radiation**.

Even 100 years after Dr. Marie Maynard Daly was born, women of color make up only about 14 percent of graduates with STEM degrees. Other diverse groups are also rare in STEM. But many organizations help to make STEM fields more diverse and inclusive for women and for other people you don't usually see in STEM careers. These groups include the Society for Advancement of Chicanos/Hispanics and Native Americans in Science (SACNAS), Association of American Indian Physicians (AAIP), National Association of Mathematicians (NAM), Out in Science, Technology, Engineering, and Mathematics (oSTEM), and the Women of Color Research Network (WOCRN).

Julian Earls received the NASA Exceptional Achievement Medal and NASA Outstanding Leadership Medal during his time with the organization.

CHAPTER 2

T Is for Technology

If you have ever watched *Star Wars* or *Lost in Space*, you've probably dreamed of going into outer space or becoming an astronaut. Or maybe you've watched planes flying overhead and wondered what it would be like to fly one. Another child who did that was Ed Dwight. When he was a boy, he dreamed of flying. After seeing Black U.S. Air Force pilot Officer Dayton Ragland, he knew he wanted to fly too.

Once realizing his dream of becoming a pilot, Dwight's career path took an exciting twist. In the early 1960s, NASA was still segregated, but military officer and pilot Dwight caught the attention of those who were considering allowing non-Whites to enter the space program. President John F. Kennedy was excited about having the first non-White man in space, and Dwight was chosen for the NASA training program.

Ed Dwight was born in 1933 in Kansas City, Kansas.

Unfortunately, the people at the program were not as excited. After President Kennedy was shot and killed, Dwight was transferred out of the program before he ever manned a rocket ship.

Although he never went to outer space, Dwight's accomplishments were many. He was a U.S. Air Force captain, a test pilot, and earned a bachelor's degree in aeronautical engineering, graduating at the top of his class.

Ed Dwight did not become an astronaut. But by being a supersonic test pilot with an astronautics degree and the first Black man in the astronaut training program, he inspired many and paved the way for many others.

Two Passions

Although Ed Dwight did not make it to outer space, he was able to follow his other love, art. He has completed many commissioned works. One, a series of sculptures about Black people who settled in the West, taught viewers about a diverse Wild West unknown to most. Dwight also completed statues showing the evolution of jazz. One of his most notable works is an inaugural scene featuring all four members of the Obama family. Learn more about his work at EdDwight.com.

Becoming an astronaut wasn't a real possibility for everybody until about 40 years ago. Until 1978, the NASA program was largely closed to anyone who was not White and male. After 1978, NASA began to take diversity more seriously. Finally, people like Guy Bluford and Mae Jemison were able to become the first Black man and the first Black woman to travel into outer space.

CHAPTER 3

E Is for Engineering

If you've ever ridden safely on a train, public transit system, or even a roller coaster, you can thank Granville T. Woods. Although popular records say he was born in Columbus, Ohio, in 1856, Woods's death certificate shows that he was born in Melbourne, Australia. Records show that he was a descendent of Aborigines, Native Americans, and African Americans.

Woods had to go to work at age 10 to help his family earn money for food, clothing, and shelter. Although he couldn't afford to go to school, he worked as an apprentice with the railroad company. As an apprentice, Woods learned the skills of a blacksmith. Blacksmiths are skilled in forming items from iron and steel. Woods also learned useful skills as a machine builder. According to reports, he was talented and was able to get college-level training in electronics, physics, and mechanical engineering after moving and living for a time in New York.

People have been using blacksmithing techniques since 1500 BCE.

With his innovation, training, and talent, Woods began to tinker at a very early age. You may have tinkered too if you've ever taken something apart to figure out how to put it back together again. Woods tinkered with machines and electronics. One of his first moneymaking inventions was an invention that combined the characteristics of the telephone and the telegraph. He called it telegraphony. This patent was later bought by Alexander Graham Bell, inventor of the telephone.

Black newspapers of the day show that Woods was known as a great inventor. So great, in fact, that he was given the nickname "Black Edison." Thomas Edison, inventor of the lightbulb, even tried to take credit for Woods's work twice. Twice Woods went to court with Edison, and twice Woods won.

At the time of his death at age 53, Granville Tailer Woods held more than 60 patents, which was exceptional for anyone. It was especially exceptional for a Black man in the segregated 1900s.

During enslavement, learning to read was dangerous, but there were some Black enclaves that taught and encouraged reading.

In the period of enslavement, during which Woods was born, learning to read or write was a crime for enslaved Africans and their descendants. In many cases, people who tried to teach enslaved Black people to read could also be punished. Keeping slaves uneducated meant they were totally dependent on their enslavers and less likely to stand up for their human rights.

GRANVILLE T. WOODS.

In 1888, Woods bought a first-class train ticket from Cincinnati, Ohio, to Nashville, Tennessee. The train ride went comfortably until the train crew changed in Kentucky. Once Woods arrived in the segregated South, the crew tried to put him off the train, because Black people could not ride in first class. When Woods stood up for his rights, the train officers violently attacked and beat him. Sadly, they did not know that the train industry owed a great debt to Granville T. Woods.

Woods's most famous inventions allowed for safe electrical train, subway, and roller coaster rides. Before Woods's inventions, wires exposed to weather could cause the aboveground railway system to be out of service for far too long. Woods's invention allowed the New York cable transit cars to be converted to wireless, electrical traction cars. In 1892 he tested his system on an early roller coaster at the Coney Island amusement park in New York City.

Also, long-distance trains sometimes had horrible crashes because there was no communication between them. Woods invented a system to allow moving trains to communicate with the station. The invention was called the Synchronous Multiplex Railway Telegraph. This system tracked trains so that they would not crash into each other. You could say Granville Woods invented wireless service, starting with trains and cable cars!

Even though most STEM experts go to school to become experts, that isn't always possible in many countries. Kelvin Doe was born in Sierra Leone in 1996. Sierra Leone is one of the poorest countries in the world. Its residents struggle to get basic food and shelter. In Sierra Leone, many people cannot go to school or college, so they teach themselves. Kelvin Doe taught himself engineering. Using scraps he found around his village, he made useful inventions. These included a battery to power lights and an FM transmitter so that he could become a disc jockey on the radio in his area.

Doe has gone to Massachusetts Institute of Technology (MIT) as its youngest visiting student. He's given lectures and speeches to people all over the world. He now heads his own company in Canada and hopes to become president of his home country someday. You can read his tweets to find out what he is doing today.

Doe is an engineer, but he also has a passion for music. He performs under the name DJ Focus.

CHAPTER 4

M Is for Math

You probably have played *Cool Math Games* on your computer, but do you understand how cool math really is? Dr. Tai-Danae Bradley is dedicated to helping both people who love math and those who struggle with the subject see math in a whole new light. Dr. Bradley is a mathematician, author, researcher, and content creator. She uses drawings and social media to promote understanding of concepts such as category theory or the relationship between algebra and statistics. When you get to college, you will learn that algebra and statistics are two very different math courses!

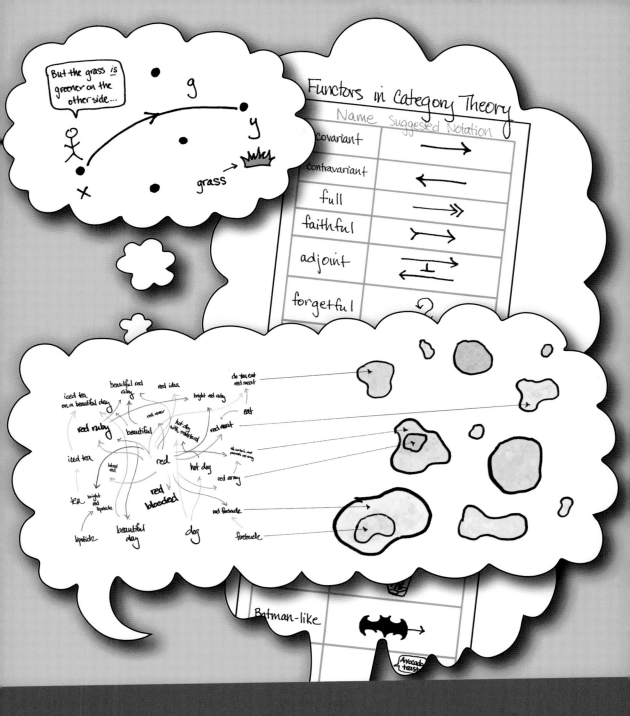

The notes seen here are from Dr. Bradley's own notebooks!

Category theory is a kind of math that helps explain relationships between different types of math. For example, in school you first take mathematics, followed by algebra, and then geometry. Once you get to college, you might take probability or statistics. These are all different specializations, much like teachers teach English or science or social studies. But mathematicians like Bradley explore not just how the fields are different, but also how they are alike and where they connect.

Often, when we think about people in math careers, we envision men. And usually older, White men. But Dr. Bradley, who graduated in 2020, shows that anyone can succeed in math. She played college basketball for two years and planned to work in athletics. But her calculus teacher inspired her to major in math instead.

Hidden Figures No Longer

Of course, Tai-Danae Bradley is just one in a long line of very cool math women. For example, if you've heard of the movie *Hidden Figures*, you may know about Katherine Johnson, Dorothy Vaughan, and Mary Jackson. These women were the mathematicians who helped NASA complete the first U.S. human flight into outer space.

Before there were computers, people did complex mathematical computing. These three women worked in a segregated area for NASA until the extraordinary value of what they did finally came to light. Johnson, Vaughan, and Jackson overcame the barriers of race and gender to become researchers, engineers, programmers, and activists. Their actions helped other Black female "human computers" achieve their educational and career goals in math, computer science, and engineering.

Currently working with Alphabet Inc., and previously with the Google Moonshot Factory, Bradley is considered a rising star in the math field. You can learn more about cool math on her PBS YouTube show *Infinite Series*. On the show, cool math topics like *The Assassin's Puzzle* and *The Honeycombs of 4-Dimensional Bees* get up to 950,000 views.

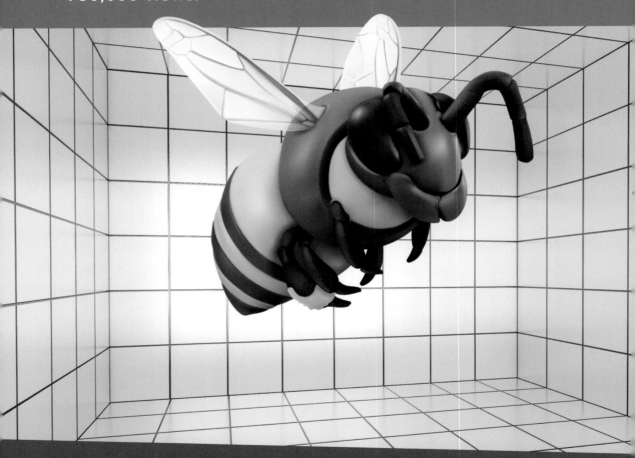

Bradley works to make mathematical concepts and theories approachable on her show *Infinite Series*.

Making a Way Out of NO WAY!!!

Journaling Your Way to Justice!

Have you ever heard of a vision board? People create vision boards to set goals for their future. You can do the same thing by creating a Justice Journal! In your Justice Journal, you can write your way to a better future for everyone.

Start by taking a notebook and adding things to the cover that represent the kind of world you want to see. You can use magazine clippings, crayons, markers, colored pencils, or words. Just be creative in designing your Justice Journal. It's a place where you will write about the world you want to see and then make a plan to create it!

As we have learned, Black people have made significant contributions in STEM in the face of adversity. They tinkered, invented, and taught themselves about science, technology, engineering, and math. In what ways do you see yourself as a scientist, technologist, engineer, or mathematician? What experiments would you try? How could you use STEM to change the world?

Write or draw in your Justice Journal and create a vision for your future. Dream big!!!

EXTEND YOUR LEARNING

Learn about the real hidden figures, NASA's human computers, in Margot Lee Shetterly's *Hidden Figures Young Readers' Edition*.

Learn more about Black heroes in STEM.
www.osc.org/black-innovators-in-stem-who-changed-the-world

GLOSSARY

Aborigines (ah-buh-RIJ-uh-neez) the people who lived in Australia before it was conquered by Europeans

acronym (AH-kruh-nim) an abbreviation that makes a commonly used word

apprentice (uh-PREHN-tuhss) a person who completes on-the-job training to learn a skill

category theory (KAH-tuh-gohr-ee THEE-uh-ree) a theory that identifies and organizes patterns and relationships between mathematical concepts

cholesterol (kuh-LEH-stuh-rohl) a waxy, fatty substance in the blood

patent (PAH-tuhnt) the right given by the government to own and make money from personal inventions; a copyright for inventors

radiation (ray-dee-AY-shuhn) process of sending out radiant energy in the form of rays or particles

segregated (seh-grih-GAY-tuhd) legal separation of Black and White citizens in public places such as restaurants, schools, and parks; also known as apartheid

traction cars (TRAK-shuhn KARZ) public transit vehicles powered by electric lines above the cars

INDEX

aeronautics, 14–16, 29
artists, 7, 17
associations and organizations, 12
astronaut training, 14, 16, 17

Bell, Alexander Graham, 20
blacksmithing, 18, 19
Bluford, Guy, 17
Bradley, Tai-Danae, 26–28, 30

category theory, 26–28
chemists, 8–9, 11
college education and degrees
    engineers, 18–19, 24
    science and scientists, 8, 12
communication systems, 20, 23, 24
computing, 29

Daly, Marie Maynard, 8–9, 11
da Vinci, Leonardo, 7
diversity and inclusion
    NASA, 17, 29
    STEM field, 12
DNA, 10, 11
doctors, 8
Doe, Kelvin, 24–25
Dwight, Ed, 14–17

Earls, Julian Manly, 12
Edison, Thomas, 20
educational attainment
    engineers, 18–19, 24
    during enslavement, 21
    literacy, 21
    math tools, 26, 28, 30
    scientists, 8, 12
engineering, 18–25
engineers, 18–20, 22–23, 24–25
enslavement, 21

Hidden Figures (film), 29

intellectual property, 20
inventors, 5, 20, 22–23, 24

Jackson, Mary, 29
Jemison, Mae, 17
Johnson, Katherine, 29
journaling, 31

Kennedy, John F., 14, 16

life sciences, 11
literacy education, 21

math, 26–30
mathematicians, 26, 28, 29, 30
military sciences, 14, 16

NASA, 12–13, 14, 16, 17, 29
notes, 7, 27

patents, 20
pilots, 14–16

racial segregation, 14, 22, 29
Ragland, Dayton, 14
railroads, 18, 22–23
reading, education, 21

science, 6–13
scientists, 6–9, 11–13
segregation, 14, 22, 29
Sierra Leone, 24
slavery, 21
space science and exploration, 12, 13, 14–16, 17, 29
STEM
    defined, 4
    engineering, 18–25
    math, 26–30
    science, 6–13
    technology, 14–17

technology, 14–17
telegraph systems, 20, 23
test pilots, 14–16
trains, 22–23
transportation technology, 18, 22–23

Vaughan, Dorothy, 29
vision boards, 31

women in STEM
    math, 26–29
    organizations, 12
    science, 8–9, 11, 12
    space science and travel, 17, 29
Woods, Granville T., 18–20, 22–23